THE PRESIDE

A good policeman is always asking questions. What happened? Why did it happen? Who did it? When? Where? Why? And a good policeman knows which answers are right, and which are wrong.

Felix is a good policeman, and the Chief of Police wants him to find a murderer. A very important murderer – the man who murdered the President. Felix must find the murderer quickly and bring him back – dead or alive. He works day and night, drives up and down the country, and asks a lot of questions.

But some questions can be dangerous. It is better not to know the answers. And dead men, of course, cannot ask, or answer, questions . . .

OXFORD BOOKWORMS LIBRARY
Thriller & Adventure

The President's Murderer

Stage 1 (400 headwords)

Series Editor: Jennifer Bassett
Founder Editor: Tricia Hedge
Activities Editors: Jennifer Bassett and Alison Baxter

JENNIFER BASSETT

The
President's Murderer

OXFORD UNIVERSITY PRESS

OXFORD
UNIVERSITY PRESS

Great Clarendon Street, Oxford OX2 6DP

Oxford University Press is a department of the University of Oxford.
It furthers the University's objective of excellence in research, scholarship,
and education by publishing worldwide in

Oxford New York

Auckland Cape Town Dar es Salaam Hong Kong Karachi
Kuala Lumpur Madrid Melbourne Mexico City Nairobi
New Delhi Shanghai Taipei Toronto

With offices in

Argentina Austria Brazil Chile Czech Republic France Greece
Guatemala Hungary Italy Japan Poland Portugal Singapore
South Korea Switzerland Thailand Turkey Ukraine Vietnam

OXFORD and OXFORD ENGLISH are registered trade marks of
Oxford University Press in the UK and in certain other countries

ISBN 978 0 19 478917 2

A complete recording of this Bookworms edition of
The President's Murderer is available on audio CD ISBN 978 0 19 478852 6

Printed in Hong Kong

Illustrated by: Paul Dickinson

Word count (main text): 5270 words

For more information on the Oxford Bookworms Library,
visit www.oup.com/elt/bookworms

CONTENTS

The First Day

'Run!' the man thought. 'Move! Faster! I can't stop now.'

Over the man's head the night sky was black and cold, and in front of him were the trees. Tall, dark trees ... five hundred metres away.

'I can hide there,' the man thought. 'I can hide in those trees. They can't see me in the trees.'

He looked behind him. He could see the lights. There were five or six men. They ran fast, and their lights moved up and down. They were not far away now. He could hear their feet on the ground.

The man ran faster. His legs were tired, his body was tired. There were noises in his head, he could not see. The trees were two hundred metres away. He wanted to stop running. He wanted to lie down and sleep.

Then he heard a new noise. Dogs.

'They've got dogs!' he thought. 'Oh no! Not dogs! I can't run faster.'

But he did. Faster and faster. The trees were a hundred metres away ... fifty ... twenty ...

And then he was there. The trees opened their dark arms to him. But he did not stop running. It was dark and

1

The trees were a hundred metres away... fifty... twenty...

quiet under the trees. He ran first to the left, and then to the right. He came to a hill, and for a second or two he stopped and listened.

Nothing. Then he heard the dogs again, but he could not see the lights.

'Don't stop now,' he thought. 'Dogs don't need eyes. They can find you in the dark.'

Quickly he ran down the hill. It was very dark here, and he could not see very well. He ran into a tree and nearly broke his arm.

'Careful!' he thought. 'Careful.' He put his hands out

2

in front of him, and ran more slowly. Then he heard a new noise. Water.

'A river!' he thought. 'The dogs can't follow me across water. Where is it? Quick!'

Soon he found the river. It was not very big, but it ran quickly. The water was cold on his tired legs. He walked and ran up the river, through the water, for about two kilometres. Then he stopped and listened again.

He could hear nothing. He stood there and waited. The trees watched him with dark, secret eyes.

Nothing. No dogs, no lights, no noises.

The man was cold now, and very, very tired. 'I need sleep,' he thought. 'Where can I hide?' He looked up at the trees.

'Up there,' he thought. 'The dogs can't follow me up a tree.'

He found a tall tree and went up it. He could not see the ground now. He half-sat, half-stood in the tree, and listened. Nothing.

'An hour,' he thought. 'Sleep for an hour. Then go on. Go south. Hide in the day, and move at night. I can get there in five days, perhaps six.'

The man put his head down on his arms, and slept.

⊕ ⊕ ⊕

'What are you saying? You lost him?' the Chief of Police said angrily.

The young police inspector in front of her was tired. Very tired. He wanted to sit down, but people did not sit down in the Chief's office. They stood and waited, and perhaps the Chief said 'Sit down'. *Then* they sat down – but not before.

So the inspector stood. 'I'm sorry, Chief,' he said. 'We couldn't find him in the trees. We looked all night, but it was dark and ...'

The Chief of Police put her hands on the desk in front of her. 'You had five men with you, Inspector, and two dogs. And you couldn't find him!'

Eva Hine, the Chief of Police, was a tall woman of about fifty. Her eyes were grey and very cold. Dangerous

'What are you saying? You lost him?' the
Chief of Police said angrily.

eyes. When Eva Hine said 'Jump!', people jumped. They did not ask questions first.

The inspector waited, and the Chief of Police looked at him coldly. 'What are you waiting for?' she asked. 'Go out and find him! Three months ago this man – Alex Dinon – killed the President of our country. He's a murderer – a dangerous man. Twenty-four hours ago he escaped from prison, and our new President wants him back in prison – today! Now! At once!'

The inspector quickly left the room.

His name was Felix, and he was thirty-three years old. That was young for an inspector, but he was a good policeman. He liked his job, and worked long hours, but he was sometimes afraid of Eva Hine, the Chief of Police.

Ten minutes later he was back in his office, and Adam came into his room. Adam was twenty-five, and usually worked with Felix on important jobs.

'What did the Chief say?' Adam asked.

'Find Dinon quickly,' Felix said. 'So, let's begin. Have we got photographs of Dinon? And what about his family?'

Adam put some photographs on the desk. 'He's got a wife and two young children,' he said.

'Right. I want photographs on television and in all the newspapers. Four men can watch his house and family, day and night – four hours on, and four hours off. Next, I want policemen at all the airports and ...'

Adam put some photographs on the desk.

Telephones rang, and people came and went in the office. Felix and Adam worked on, late into the night.

The Second Day

THE next morning Alex Dinon was forty kilometres south of the prison. He moved quickly and stayed away from towns and villages. It was winter and the weather was cold, so there were not many people in the fields. He looked behind him often, but nobody saw him and nobody followed him.

At midday he found a quiet field and lay down under some small trees. He slept at once.

At about three o'clock Alex opened his eyes, and saw an old woman in front of him.

'What are you doing in my field, young man?' she said.

Alex sat up quickly. 'I'm sorry,' he said. 'I was tired, and needed some sleep. I'm going now.'

'You're very dirty,' the old woman said. 'Look at you! Where are you going?'

'North,' Alex said. He stood up and began to move away.

'Don't run away. I'm only an old woman.' She looked at him carefully. 'You're dirty, and hungry, and tired …

8

'What are you doing in my field, young man?'
the old woman said.

and afraid. Am I right?'

Alex smiled slowly. 'Yes,' he said.

'Well, come back to my house and have some food. And you can have some of my husband's old clothes. He died last winter.'

Alex looked at her. It was true. He was hungry and tired and dirty. And afraid ... but not of this old woman. 'Thank you very much,' he said.

The old woman's name was Marta. Her house was very small, but she put some wonderful hot food in front of Alex. He ate quickly, and Marta watched him.

'Oh, you *were* hungry,' she laughed.

Alex smiled, but did not stop eating.

Marta found some old clothes for him, and then made some coffee. She said nothing, but watched him with a smile. Alex finished eating and drank some coffee. He began to feel better.

'How did you escape from prison?' Marta asked suddenly.

Alex's face went white. He stared at Marta and said nothing.

Marta laughed. 'It's all right,' she said. 'I'm not afraid of the President's murderer. You can stay here tonight, Alex Dinon, and have a good sleep. I don't like the police, and I'm not going to tell them.'

⊕ ⊕ ⊕

'How did you escape from prison?' Marta asked suddenly.

Felix and Adam did not get much sleep. They stayed in the office and slept between telephone calls. The phones rang often, but in the morning there was no news of Alex Dinon. The day went slowly. The phones rang again and again – but there was no news.

'Where is he? What's he doing?' Felix said to Adam. 'He's hiding – perhaps with friends.'

'We questioned all his friends early this morning,' Adam said. 'They said nothing.' He looked at Felix. 'Can we bring some of them in here? With their wives. Then we can ask more … difficult questions. Somebody usually talks then.'

'No,' Felix said coldly. 'That's not right, and you know it. Dinon can't get out of the country now. But we need to find him today. The Chief isn't going to be very happy.'

Late in the afternoon the Chief of Police telephoned. 'Come to my office in half an hour,' she told Felix.

Felix felt tired and dirty. He quickly drank some black coffee, and changed his shirt. Twenty minutes later he stood in front of Eva Hine's desk.

She did not smile, but looked at Felix and waited.

'The police are looking for Dinon in every town and village,' Felix said quickly. 'We're watching the roads and the airports, and the houses of his family and friends …'

'Sit down, Inspector, and listen,' the Chief said. 'We need to find this man quickly. The President is not happy.

12

You're a good policeman, Inspector, and this is an important job for you.'

'Chief,' Felix began. 'How did Dinon escape from prison?'

'That's not important now,' the Chief said.

'But perhaps he had friends in prison,' Felix said. 'Perhaps they know something. I need to talk to people at the prison.'

'Well, you can't,' the Chief said.

The telephone rang on the Chief's desk. She picked up the phone. 'Eva Hine here.' Then she smiled. 'Yes, Mr President,' she said. She listened for a minute or two. 'Yes, of course, Mr President. I understand. Yes. Goodbye.'

Eva Hine put the phone down and looked at Felix angrily. 'Forget Dinon's escape from prison. Get out there and find him. And bring him back dead or alive!'

At the door Felix turned and looked at her. 'Dead?' he asked slowly.

'Dead men can't talk. Now go!'

Felix walked slowly back to his office. There were a lot of questions in his head, and he did not know the answers. 'Why can't I talk to people at the prison?' he thought. 'What did the President say to the Chief on the phone? And why does she want Dinon dead? He went to prison because he murdered the old President. Everybody knows that. What can he talk about … now?'

'And bring Dinon back dead or alive!' Eva Hine said.

The Third Day

ALEX slept well for many hours, and the next morning Marta put a big breakfast on the table. Alex ate hungrily, and Marta talked.

'What's happening to this country?' she said. 'I don't know. I didn't like the old President. He was old and stupid. There's never much food in the shops. When did I last eat some good meat?' she said angrily. 'I work every day, and what do I get? Nothing!'

'What do you think about the new President, then?' Alex asked.

'Oh, he's worse! He's a younger man, and he's not stupid, but he's more dangerous. He's very friendly with the police and the army. And he's putting a lot of people in prison. That's not good for the country. We want more food, not more prisoners.'

Just then they heard somebody at the door.

'Quick!' Marta said. 'Upstairs. Hide under the bed.'

Alex ran upstairs and hid. Three minutes later Marta came quickly upstairs. Her face was very angry.

'That was my friend George from the house down the road. Somebody saw you at the window this morning. It was that woman from the post office. The police give her

15

money, and she tells them all the secrets of the village. Everybody hates her!'

'The police always have a "friend" in every village,' Alex said sadly. 'Marta, I'm going now. At once. The police are going to be here soon, and ...'

'Huh!' Marta said angrily. 'I'm not afraid of the police or their questions. Alex Dinon? Who's he? Is he somebody on television?'

Alex smiled. 'You're a wonderful woman, Marta,' he said. 'Goodbye, and thank you.'

Marta looked at Alex and her old face was suddenly unhappy. 'Good luck, boy,' she said.

Alex left the house quickly. He went through Marta's back garden, and out into the fields again. He felt better after the night in Marta's house. He thought about Marta and smiled. Boy! He was thirty-three years old and a "dangerous murderer", but to Marta he was only a tired and hungry boy.

⊕ ⊕ ⊕

At eight o'clock in the morning of the third day the telephone rang on Felix's desk. Felix listened, then put the phone down quickly.

'Adam!' he shouted. 'We've got him! He's in a village up north. In an old woman's house. Come on. Let's go!'

The big police car was fast, and the kilometres went

16

'You're a wonderful woman Marta,' Alex said.
'Goodbye, and thank you.'

quickly. Adam was tired and wanted to sleep, but Felix wanted to talk. 'I saw the Chief again last night,' he said. 'She's getting angry. I was in her office and the President phoned her. They want Dinon badly – dead or alive. Why do they want him dead?'

'I don't know,' Adam said. 'Let's find him first.'

In Marta's village a policeman stood at the door of her house. 'We looked all through the house, and there's nobody in there,' he said. 'Only Marta, the old woman. And she's not talking.'

Felix, Adam and the policeman went into the house. 'Hello!' Marta said. 'More policemen? What an exciting day!'

'Listen to the Inspector,' Adam said angrily. 'He wants to ask you some questions.'

Felix sat down and smiled at Marta. 'Now, Marta,' he said. 'Somebody saw a young man in your house yesterday. Who was he, Marta, and where did he go?'

'He was my sister's youngest son,' Marta said happily. 'He's a very nice boy.'

The policeman whispered in Felix's ear. Felix looked sadly at Marta. 'Your sister and all her family live in Australia, Marta. Who was the man in your house?'

'Oh dear!' Marta said. 'I'm an old woman, you know. Seventy-two last month. I forget things very easily. In Australia, did you say?'

18

Felix asked question after question, but Marta told him nothing. Sometimes the young man in her house was her sister's son. Sometimes he was the young doctor from the next village, but he was never Alex Dinon, the President's murderer. Adam got very angry and whispered to Felix:

'Can I ask the questions?'

'No,' Felix said. He did not like Adam's questions. He stood up and moved to the door, but Marta now wanted to ask him a question:

'And why do you work for the police, young man? The police always put the wrong people in prison, you know.'

'Marta,' Felix said tiredly, 'Alex Dinon is a murderer. He murdered—'

'Oh, I know that,' Marta said. 'The newspapers said that. But newspapers and the television never tell us the true story. Alex Dinon isn't a murderer. He's a nice young man.'

'A nice young man?' Felix said quickly. 'How do you know that?'

'He's got a nice face. That's why. I saw his picture on the television. I'm an old woman and I can read people's faces.'

'So who *did* murder the President, then?' Felix asked.

'I don't know,' Marta said. '*You're* the policeman. *You* go and find the murderer. But I can tell you one thing. You can begin with the new President. *He's* got a murderer's face.'

19

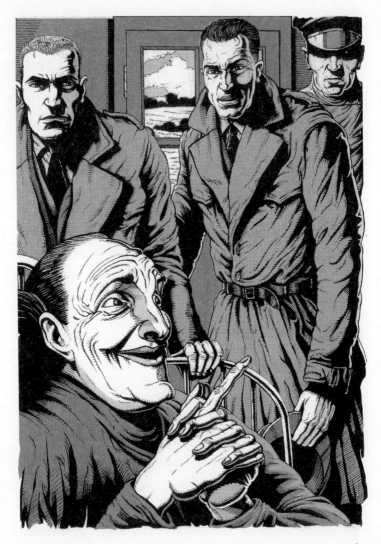

'And why do you work for the police, young man?' Marta said.

Adam said angrily, 'That's dangerous talk.'

Marta laughed, and Felix opened the door. 'Let's go, Adam,' he said quietly.

Out in the road Adam said, 'Stupid old woman!'

'Yes,' Felix said. 'Perhaps she was ... and perhaps she wasn't.'

The Fourth Day

AFTER he left Marta's village, Alex moved quickly and quietly across the fields. Nobody saw him. He walked and ran, and walked again. It rained all day and all night. He walked through the night, and the next morning – the fourth day – he was very tired and very hungry. He hid in some trees for an hour or two, then he went on south. Always south. To his home town.

'Where can I go?' he thought. 'Perhaps I can escape from the country, but I want to see Olivia again before I leave ... or before the police find me.'

But first he needed food. He had some money in his pocket – Marta's money. He remembered her words. *You take it. I don't need it. An old woman doesn't need money.* Alex smiled. What a wonderful old woman!

He came to a small town on a river, and found a food

shop in a quiet street. He opened the door and went in. There were a lot of people in the shop, and he waited quietly behind them. People looked at him, and a man went out quickly. Alex wanted to run, but he was very hungry, so he waited. Then a woman with her young son came into the shop. The woman whispered to the boy, and the boy came up to Alex. 'There are two policemen in the street,' he said very quietly, 'and they're coming here.'

Alex looked quickly at the door, but he could not escape now. Then the shopkeeper called to him, 'Hey, you!' he said. 'Quick! Go out through the back.'

Alex ran through the back of the shop, and the shopkeeper followed him. 'I never help the police – they're all bad,' he said. He opened the back door and looked out. 'It's OK,' he said quickly. 'You can get out of town along the river. Follow the back of the houses. Nobody goes there. Good luck!'

'Thank you,' Alex said, and ran.

Three kilometres from the town Alex came to a road. He crossed the road quickly but a lorry came along at the same time. The lorry slowed down and the driver called out to him, 'Where are you going?'

Alex said the name of his home town, and the driver said, 'Come on. I'm going near there. You can come with me.'

Alex got into the front of the lorry, and the driver

22

The woman whispered to the boy, and the boy came up to Alex.

looked carefully into his face. 'Do I know you?' he asked.

Alex said nothing, and waited. He felt very tired. The driver stared at him for a minute, then he smiled. 'No, I don't know you,' he said. 'Get into the back of the lorry. Nobody can see you there. Are you hungry?'

'Yes, I am,' Alex said. 'Very.'

'Well, I've got some sandwiches. Here you are. Now, get in the back quickly. Before we see a police car.'

The lorry drove slowly south. Alex ate all the driver's sandwiches and then slept like a dead man.

⊕ ⊕ ⊕

'We're always three hours or more behind him,' Felix said to Adam in the car. 'We drive up and down the country, but Dinon always moves on before we get there.'

'Perhaps this shopkeeper can tell us something,' Adam said.

But the shopkeeper was not helpful. 'Alex who?' he said.

'DINON!' Felix shouted. He was very tired. 'He escaped from prison five days ago. Somebody saw him in your shop.'

'I don't have prisoners in my shop,' the shopkeeper said angrily. 'And I don't want the police here.'

'*Did* Dinon come into this shop?' Felix asked.

'Dinon,' the shopkeeper said slowly. 'What did he do?

The lorry driver smiled. 'No, I don't know you,' he said.

Wait a minute. Yes! Did he write a book about the old President?'

'He *killed* the President,' Adam said. 'He murdered him.'

'Oh yes,' the shopkeeper said. 'I remember now. It was a good book. But the President's murderer did not come into my shop this morning.'

Felix watched the shopkeeper's face carefully. 'My question', he said, 'asked about Alex Dinon.'

The shopkeeper looked at Felix and smiled slowly. 'That's right,' he said.

Felix and Adam talked to a lot of people and asked a lot of questions in that small town, but they learned nothing.

Later, back in the office, Felix was very quiet. Suddenly he looked at Adam across the desk, and said:

'We can't get Dinon's book in this country. Do you know it, Adam?'

'No,' Adam said.

Felix stared at the telephone on his desk. 'Where *is* Dinon?' he said slowly. 'People are helping him, but why? He's a murderer. And nobody wants to help us.'

'People never help the police in this country,' Adam said. 'People don't like us.'

'Why are we policemen, Adam?'

'It's a good job,' Adam said. 'And the money's good.'

Felix and Adam asked a lot of questions in that small town, but they learned nothing.

After a minute or two Felix said, 'Did Dinon murder the President? What do you think, Adam?'

'Well, why did they put him in prison, then?'

'That doesn't answer my question,' Felix said.

'I do my job,' Adam said, 'and I don't ask questions.'

Felix looked at him, but said nothing.

The Fifth Day

IN an old house in a quiet road a woman waited. She waited day and night, and did not sleep. At nine o'clock in the evening of the fifth day, she heard a noise at the window at the back of the house.

Quickly, she ran and opened the window. A minute later she was in Alex's arms. They did not speak for a long time.

Then they talked quietly about their friends and their family. 'The children are with my sister,' Olivia said. 'It's better for them there. But I came here to Rudi's house. Rudi's away, and Pauli told me this was the best place to wait. I wanted to see you before you leave the country. Oh Alex, I'm so afraid for you.'

'Yes, escape is going to be difficult,' Alex said. 'I talked to Pauli on the phone. The police …'

'Yes, but you escaped from prison,' Olivia said quickly. 'You have a lot of friends. Perhaps Pauli can help you. Or ...'

'Perhaps. I've got some good friends. I know that. But I've got a lot of enemies too,' Alex said slowly. 'Very dangerous enemies.'

Suddenly Olivia saw his hands. 'Your hands! Oh Alex, what happened to your hands?'

Alex looked down at them. 'It happened in prison,' he said slowly. 'They did it with a knife ... and cigarettes.'

'But why?' Olivia whispered. 'Why did they do that?'

'They wanted a name, but I didn't tell them.'

'What name?'

'The name of the President's murderer.'

'But they say you killed him ...' Olivia began.

'Yes, but I did not kill the President. And the police know that.'

'So they put *you* in prison,' Olivia said, 'because they needed a murderer.'

'Yes. And because of my book about the old President, and the government of this country. It was a very angry book. Do you remember?' Alex smiled. 'But the old President read it, and liked it. He wasn't a bad man, and he wanted a better life for the people. He wanted to change things in this country, but he couldn't. The police and the army stopped him. And the new President, of

'But I did not kill the President,' Alex said.
'And the police know that.'

course, is a good friend of the police and the army. A very good friend.' Alex laughed angrily. 'You see, Olivia, the police *know* the murderer's name, but it's a secret. They don't want people in this country to know the name. And so they were angry with me in prison, because they think that *I* know the murderer's name.'

Olivia's face was afraid. 'Do ... Do you know?' she whispered.

'Yes.' Alex looked at his wife's white, unhappy face. 'But I'm not going to tell you,' he said quietly. 'It's a very ... dangerous name.'

Alex ate some food and changed his clothes. Then he slept, and Olivia watched the road through the windows.

⊕ ⊕ ⊕

In his office Felix waited for more news. He waited, and he thought – about his job, about the dead President and the new President, about the old woman Marta, about Eva Hine, the Chief of Police – and about Alex Dinon.

At 9.05 p.m. the telephone rang on Felix's desk. He listened, then quickly jumped to his feet and called to Adam. 'Dinon's in his home town,' he shouted. 'He's in his old teacher's house. He went in three minutes ago.'

Adam laughed. 'We've got him now,' he said happily.

'Listen,' Felix said quickly. 'Take ten more men with

you and drive down to Dinon's town at once. Wait near the house and watch, but don't go in. I'm going to phone the Chief now, and then follow you.'

'Right,' Adam said, and quickly left the room.

Felix phoned the Chief and told her the news.

'*Good,*' the Chief said. '*Now wait there. I want to speak to you again in ten minutes.*'

Felix waited angrily. He wanted to leave at once. He wanted to talk to Alex Dinon. Perhaps Dinon knew the answers to Felix's questions. The phone rang and Felix picked it up quickly.

'*Now listen, Inspector. Don't go into the house. Wait in the road and watch.*'

'But we can go into the house and get him!' Felix said. 'Why not?'

'*No, that's dangerous. Perhaps his wife and children are in the house.*'

'But his children are with his wife's sister. We know that,' Felix said. 'So ...'

'*LISTEN TO ME, INSPECTOR!*'

Felix did not answer.

'*Are you listening to me, Inspector?*'

'Yes, Chief,' Felix said quietly.

'*Now, Dinon can't stay in the house. He's going to come out later in the night, when the streets are quiet. He can't escape. The soldiers—*'

32

'*Are you listening to me, Inspector?*'
the Chief of Police said.

'Soldiers? What soldiers?' Felix said angrily. 'I don't need the army!'

'*This man Dinon is very, very important, Inspector. You need help, and the army is going to help you. They're putting three hundred men in all the roads near the house. I want Dinon tonight, Inspector!*'

The Chief put the phone down, and Felix stared at his desk. 'Alive ... or dead?' he thought. 'Which does she – and our new President – want? I think I know the answer. They want him dead. And I want to know why!'

The police car took Felix to Dinon's home town, an hour away, and Felix found Adam in a quiet street behind the house. They sat in Adam's car and talked.

Adam looked at Felix's face. 'What are you angry about?' he asked. 'Dinon's in the house. And he can't escape now. When he comes out – Wham! We've got him!'

'I'm angry,' Felix said, 'because half the army with its guns is in this town tonight. I wanted to go into the house, but I can't because the Chief said "no", and the soldiers are watching the house. But I wanted to get to Dinon first.'

'That's going to be difficult,' Adam said. 'Soldiers shoot first, and ask questions later.'

'Yes,' Felix said slowly. 'They're going to kill Alex Dinon, and I can't stop them.'

The Sixth Day

A T three o'clock in the morning Alex got up from the bed and looked out of the window. Olivia opened her eyes. 'Are you ... Are you leaving now?' she asked.

'Yes,' Alex said. 'I can't stay longer. Perhaps the police are out there now. They're watching all our friends' houses. Pauli told me.' He put on his shoes and coat, then looked at his wife.

'Olivia. Listen. Be very careful and live very quietly. The police are going to watch you for some time. Wait for a year, then take the children and leave the country secretly. Our friends can help you. Find a new home in a new country and make a new life.'

Olivia began to cry. 'But Alex! You're going to be there with us.'

Alex smiled. 'Yes. Perhaps.' He took his wife's face in his hands and looked into her unhappy eyes. 'Don't cry, my love,' he said quietly. 'Give me a smile before I go.'

'Oh Alex! I'm afraid!' Olivia could not stop crying. 'I love you, I love you,' she whispered. 'Go quickly. And be careful. Please.'

Alex smiled sadly. 'Goodbye, my love.'

He left the house quickly and went out into the dark night. He waited for ten minutes at the door and listened,

'I can't stay longer,' Alex said. 'Perhaps the police are out there now.'

but he heard nothing and saw nothing. He came out into the road very carefully. Again he waited. From an upstairs window in his house, a white face watched him.

Then Alex began to walk quickly along the road. He stayed near the houses and looked behind him again and

36

again. Two hundred metres along the road there was a car. Alex stared at it, but there was nobody in the car, and he walked quickly past.

Suddenly there were noises and lights – and soldiers with guns. Alex began to run, but he did not run far. There was a shot ... two, three, four, five shots ... And Alex did not move again.

⊕ ⊕ ⊕

Felix ran across the road and looked at the body. Adam was there before him.

'Is he alive?' Felix asked quickly.

'No, he's dead.' Adam stood up and looked at Felix. 'Very, very dead,' he said.

Felix's face was angry. 'The soldiers killed him,' he said.

Adam looked at Felix. 'Well, that's their job. Dinon ran away, so the soldiers shot him. "Alive or dead", the Chief said. But we found him. That's the important thing.'

Felix stared down at Alex Dinon's face. 'I wanted to talk to him ... to ask him ...'

'To ask him what?' Adam said.

Felix did not answer. He looked down at the dead body on the road, then he turned away.

'Nothing,' he said. 'It doesn't matter.'

There was a lot of noise in the road now. Soldiers and

Felix stared down at Alex Dinon's dead face.

policemen moved here and there. Police cars came and went. The people in the houses looked out of their windows, but they did not open their doors. It was better not to ask questions. An ambulance came and took the body away.

Later that day Felix went back to the Chief's office. The Chief called him into her room.

'So he's dead,' she said. 'Well done, Felix. The President is very pleased with you.'

The Chief did not often say 'Felix'. Usually she called him 'Inspector'.

Felix sat down and looked at Eva Hine. 'A lot of people think ...' He stopped. Then he began again. 'They say ... Alex Dinon wasn't the President's murderer.'

'People say a lot of things,' the Chief said. She smiled. 'But they're not all true. Don't listen to stories, Felix. You've got a good job. Don't ask questions.'

'But perhaps,' Felix said slowly, 'the stories are true. And it's a policeman's job to ask questions.'

Eva Hine stood up and came nearer to Felix. She looked down into his face, and her grey eyes were cold.

'Listen,' she said. 'Somebody murdered the old President. Right? And our new President needed a murderer. Quickly. So we found a murderer for him. Alex Dinon. We don't kill murderers in this country. They go to prison. But Dinon escaped from prison – and now he's dead. The murderer is dead, Felix, and that's the end of the story.'

It was very quiet in the room. The Chief watched Felix and waited. Felix looked down at his hands and said nothing. Then he looked up into Eva Hine's cold eyes.

'Who murdered the President?' he asked.

Eva Hine's face did not change. She stared at Felix, and Felix stared back at her.

After a long time Eva Hine said, 'Perhaps you need a new job, Felix. Think about it ... very carefully.'

The young man looked at her face, then he looked away, out of the window. After a minute or two he stood

'The murderer is dead, Felix, and that's the end of the story.'

up, and went to the door. Then he turned and looked at the Chief of Police.

'I'd like to know the murderer's name,' he said quietly. 'And I'm going to find it.' He opened the door. 'Goodbye, Chief.'

He went out and closed the door behind him, for the last time.

GLOSSARY

airport a place where aeroplanes can land and take off

army all the soldiers of a country

Chief (of Police) the most important person (in the police)

clothes things to wear to cover the body, e.g. dresses, shirts, trousers

dangerous something dangerous can hurt or kill you

enemy the opposite of a friend; someone who hates you or wants to hurt you

escape to get free; to run away from a place

field a piece of ground where animals eat grass, or people grow food to eat

follow to come or go after someone or something

food what you eat

government the people who control a country

ground the ground is under our feet

gun a thing that shoots out bullets to kill people

hide (past tense **hid**) to go or stay in a place where people cannot see you or find you

inspector an important policeman/woman

job work that you do for money

jump (*v*) to move quickly with both feet off the ground

lie (past tense **lay**) to put your body flat on something (e.g. a bed, the ground)

life the time when you are alive, not dead

light (*n*) to see in the dark, you need a light

lorry a big 'car' without windows which carries heavy things

murder (*v*) to kill somebody (not in an accident)

murderer a person who murders

newspaper   you read a newspaper to know what is happening in the world

police   people who look for bad people and send them to prison

president   the most important person in a government

prison   a big building for bad people; they live there and cannot leave

ring (past tense **rang**)   to make a sound like a bell (e.g. a telephone rings)

sadly   not happily

secret   something that you do not want other people to know

shoot (*v*)   to send a bullet from a gun and kill or hurt somebody

shopkeeper   a person who has a small shop

shot (*n*)   the noise when a gun is fired

shout (*v*)   to speak or cry very loudly and strongly

soldier   a man who fights for his country

stare (*v*)   to look at someone or something for a long time

stupid   not clever; with very slow thinking

turn (*v*)   to move round; to change direction

whisper (*v*)   to speak very, very quietly

The President's Murderer

ACTIVITIES

Before Reading

1 **Read the back cover and the story introduction on the first page of the book. What do you know now about this story? Tick one box for each sentence.**

	YES	NO
1 The old President is dead.	☐	☐
2 There is now a new President.	☐	☐
3 Somebody murdered the old President.	☐	☐
4 The murderer is in prison.	☐	☐
5 Felix is the Chief of Police.	☐	☐
6 Felix must find the murderer.	☐	☐
7 Felix stays in his office all day.	☐	☐
8 Felix asks some dangerous questions.	☐	☐

2 **What is going to happen in this story? Can you guess? Use this table to make some sentences.**

	shoots the running man.
Felix	leaves the country.
The Chief of Police	leaves his job.
The new President	dies.
The running man	catches the murderer.
The army	doesn't catch the murderer.
	kills the new President.

While Reading

Read *The First Day*, and then answer these questions.

1 Why did Dinon want to get to the trees?
2 Why did he walk up the river, through the water?
3 What did Dinon do three months ago?
4 What did Dinon do twenty-four hours ago?
5 What did Eva Hine want Felix to do?
6 Who worked with Felix on important jobs?

Read *The Second Day*, and choose the best words to complete these passages.

Alex *was / wasn't* afraid of Marta, so he *went / didn't go* to her house with her. He *told / didn't tell* Marta his name, but she *knew / didn't know* him. She *wanted / didn't want* to help Alex because she *liked / didn't like* the police, so Alex *stayed / didn't stay* the night in her house.

Dinon escaped from prison, but Felix *knew / didn't know* how. He *wanted / didn't want* to talk to people at the prison, but Eva Hine said that he *could / couldn't* do that. She wanted Felix to *forget / remember* Dinon's escape from prison and to *lose / find* him quickly. And she wanted Dinon *dead / alive* because dead men *could / couldn't* talk.

Read *The Third Day*, and answer these questions.

Who

1 . . . was very friendly with the police and the army?
2 . . . didn't like the old or the new President?
3 . . . told the police about a young man in Marta's house?
4 . . . told Marta about the police?
5 . . . always had a 'friend' in every village?
6 . . . was only a tired and hungry boy to Marta?
7 . . . lived in Australia?
8 . . . asked Marta a lot of questions?
9 . . . thought the new President had a murderer's face?
10 . . . thought Marta was a stupid old woman?

Before you read *The Fourth Day*, think about these questions.

1 Why do the President and Eva Hine want Dinon dead?
2 What is Felix beginning to think about Dinon?

Read *The Fourth Day*, and join these halves of sentences.

1 The next morning Alex was very hungry, . . .
2 A man quickly left the shop . . .
3 Alex escaped before the police arrived . . .
4 The lorry driver wanted to help Alex too, . . .
5 When Felix and Adam went to the shop, . . .
6 Felix and Adam asked a lot of questions in the town, . . .

7 the shopkeeper talked about Alex Dinon's book.

8 because a small boy and the shopkeeper helped him.

9 so he went into a food shop in a small town.

10 but nobody told them anything.

11 and Alex went south in the back of his lorry.

12 and went to tell the police about Alex.

Read *The Fifth Day*. Are these sentences true (T) or false (F)? Change the false sentences into true ones.

1 Olivia wanted Alex to stay in the country.

2 Alex killed the President and the police knew that.

3 The old President read Alex's book and liked it.

4 The police didn't know the murderer's name.

5 Alex knew the murderer's name.

6 Felix phoned the President and he phoned the Chief.

7 Felix wanted the army's help and he was pleased about the soldiers.

8 Felix wanted to talk to Alex Dinon.

Before you read the last chapter (*The Sixth Day*), can you guess the answers to these questions?

1 What question does Felix want to ask Alex Dinon?

2 Do the soldiers shoot Alex?

3 Does Felix get to Alex first and ask his question?

4 What does Felix do next?

After Reading

1 **Look at these headlines in the newspapers on the day after Alex Dinon died. Which ones are nearest to the *true* story?**

DANGEROUS MURDERER DEAD

DINON DEAD: A HAPPY DAY FOR OUR PRESIDENT

SOLDIERS SHOOT AN ENEMY OF OUR COUNTRY

DEAD MEN CANNOT TALK, MR PRESIDENT

2 **After Alex died, Marta wrote to Olivia. Complete her letter with these words. (Use each word once.)**

better, change, enemy, escaped, field, food, good, government, house, know, murderer, newspapers, prison, soldiers, sorry

Dear Mrs Dinon

You don't _____ me, but I met your husband soon after he _____ from _____. I found him in my _____, took him to my _____, and gave him some good hot _____. Today the _____ say that the _____ killed him. I am so _____, Mrs Dinon. Your husband wasn't a _____, or an _____ of the country. Everybody knows that, and we don't listen to the _____. Your husband wanted to _____ things and give us all a _____ life. He was a _____ man.

From a friend

3 **Before Eva Hine phoned Felix back (see page 32), she talked to the President. Put their conversation in the right order and write in the speakers' names. Eva Hine speaks first (number 5).**

1 _____ 'In front of his wife? No, that doesn't look good. We need a better story than that. Think, Eva, think.'

2 _____ 'In his home town – in his old teacher's house.'

3 _____ '. . . but of course he doesn't stop . . .'

4 _____ 'Yes, Mr President. Right. I'm thinking. How about this? We put the army in the streets, and wait. Dinon must move on. So, later in the night, when everything is quiet, he leaves the house.'

5 _____ 'Mr President, I have some news about Dinon.'

6 _____ 'Yes, Eva, I like that story. I like it very much. Do it. And phone me when he's dead.'

7 _____ 'Good. Where is he?'

8 _____ 'So, do we go in and shoot him?'

9 _____ '. . . and so the soldiers shoot him.'

10 _____ 'I like the beginning, Eva. What happens next?'

11 _____ 'Yes. We think his wife's there too. What do you want me to do now, Mr President?'

12 _____ 'He is afraid. Perhaps he hears something. He begins to run. The soldiers shout "Stop!", . . .'

13 _____ 'I told you, Eva. I want this man dead.'

14 _____ 'Is there anybody with him in the house?'

4 Here is a new illustration for the story. Find the best place in the story to put the picture, and answer these questions.

The picture goes on page ____.
1   Who are the two men in this picture?
2   Which man is leaving, and why?
3   Why is the second man helping him?

Now write a caption for the illustration.

Caption: _____

5 Look at these questions about Felix and Adam, and talk about your answers.

1 Who said: '*I do my job, and don't ask questions*'?
2 Who said: '*It's a policeman's job to ask questions*'?
3 What do these words tell us about Felix and Adam?
4 Which man was the better policeman?

6 So who did kill the President? What do *you* think? Choose one of these answers, and explain why.

Alex Dinon / one of Dinon's friends / Eva Hine / the army / the new President / one of the new President's friends

7 Does Felix ever learn the murderer's name? Choose words from A, B, and C to make some new endings for the story.

A • Felix never learns the murderer's name.
  • Felix learns the murderer's name.
B • Eva Hine tries to kill him, . . .
  • He stops asking dangerous questions, . . .
  • The next day he dies suddenly, in an 'accident', . . .
  • He doesn't tell anyone, . . .
  • He tells the newspapers and people are very angry.
C • and years later, he gets the Chief of Police's job.
  • so nobody ever learns the true story.
  • Soon there is a new government in the country.
  • and Dinon's friends help him to leave the country.

ABOUT THE AUTHOR

Jennifer Bassett has worked in English Language Teaching since 1972. She has been a teacher, teacher trainer, editor, and materials writer, and has taught in England, Greece, Spain, and Portugal. She is the current Series Editor of the Oxford Bookworms Library, and has written several other stories for the series, including *One-Way Ticket* and *The Phantom of the Opera* (both at Stage 1).

Jennifer Bassett lives and works in Devonshire, in the south-west of England. She enjoys going for long walks across the quiet Devon hills, and often thinks of plots for stories while she is walking.

OXFORD BOOKWORMS LIBRARY

Classics • Crime & Mystery • Factfiles • Fantasy & Horror
Human Interest • Playscripts • Thriller & Adventure
True Stories • World Stories

The OXFORD BOOKWORMS LIBRARY provides enjoyable reading in English, with a wide range of classic and modern fiction, non-fiction, and plays. It includes original and adapted texts in seven carefully graded language stages, which take learners from beginner to advanced level. An overview is given on the next pages.

All Stage 1 titles are available as audio recordings, as well as over eighty other titles from Starter to Stage 6. All Starters and many titles at Stages 1 to 4 are specially recommended for younger learners. Every Bookworm is illustrated, and Starters and Factfiles have full-colour illustrations.

The OXFORD BOOKWORMS LIBRARY also offers extensive support. Each book contains an introduction to the story, notes about the author, a glossary, and activities. Additional resources include tests and worksheets, and answers for these and for the activities in the books. There is advice on running a class library, using audio recordings, and the many ways of using Oxford Bookworms in reading programmes. Resource materials are available on the website <www.oup.com/elt/bookworms>.

The *Oxford Bookworms Collection* is a series for advanced learners. It consists of volumes of short stories by well-known authors, both classic and modern. Texts are not abridged or adapted in any way, but carefully selected to be accessible to the advanced student.

You can find details and a full list of titles in the *Oxford Bookworms Library Catalogue* and *Oxford English Language Teaching Catalogues*, and on the website <www.oup.com/elt/bookworms>.

THE OXFORD BOOKWORMS LIBRARY
GRADING AND SAMPLE EXTRACTS

STARTER • 250 HEADWORDS

present simple – present continuous – imperative –
can/cannot, must – *going to* (future) – simple gerunds …

Her phone is ringing – but where is it?

Sally gets out of bed and looks in her bag. No phone. She looks under the bed. No phone. Then she looks behind the door. There is her phone. Sally picks up her phone and answers it. *Sally's Phone*

STAGE 1 • 400 HEADWORDS

… past simple – coordination with *and*, *but*, *or* –
subordination with *before*, *after*, *when*, *because*, *so* …

I knew him in Persia. He was a famous builder and I worked with him there. For a time I was his friend, but not for long. When he came to Paris, I came after him – I wanted to watch him. He was a very clever, very dangerous man. *The Phantom of the Opera*

STAGE 2 • 700 HEADWORDS

… present perfect – *will* (future) – *(don't) have to, must not, could* –
comparison of adjectives – simple *if* clauses – past continuous –
tag questions – *ask/tell* + infinitive …

While I was writing these words in my diary, I decided what to do. I must try to escape. I shall try to get down the wall outside. The window is high above the ground, but I have to try. I shall take some of the gold with me – if I escape, perhaps it will be helpful later. *Dracula*

STAGE 3 • 1000 HEADWORDS

... should, may – present perfect continuous – *used to* – past perfect –
causative – relative clauses – indirect statements ...

Of course, it was most important that no one should see
Colin, Mary, or Dickon entering the secret garden. So Colin
gave orders to the gardeners that they must all keep away
from that part of the garden in future. *The Secret Garden*

STAGE 4 • 1400 HEADWORDS

... past perfect continuous – passive (simple forms) –
would conditional clauses – indirect questions –
relatives with *where/when* – gerunds after prepositions/phrases ...

I was glad. Now Hyde could not show his face to the world
again. If he did, every honest man in London would be proud
to report him to the police. *Dr Jekyll and Mr Hyde*

STAGE 5 • 1800 HEADWORDS

... future continuous – future perfect –
passive (modals, continuous forms) –
would have conditional clauses – modals + perfect infinitive ...

If he had spoken Estella's name, I would have hit him. I was so
angry with him, and so depressed about my future, that I could
not eat the breakfast. Instead I went straight to the old house.
Great Expectations

STAGE 6 • 2500 HEADWORDS

... passive (infinitives, gerunds) – advanced modal meanings –
clauses of concession, condition

When I stepped up to the piano, I was confident. It was as if I
knew that the prodigy side of me really did exist. And when I
started to play, I was so caught up in how lovely I looked that
I didn't worry how I would sound. *The Joy Luck Club*

Sherlock Holmes and the Sport of Kings

SIR ARTHUR CONAN DOYLE

Retold by Jennifer Bassett

Horseracing is the sport of kings, perhaps because racehorses are very expensive animals. But when they win races, they can make a lot of money too – money for the owners, for the trainers, and for the people who put bets on them to win.

Silver Blaze is a young horse, but already the winner of many races. One night he disappears from his stables, and someone kills his trainer. The police want the killer, and the owner wants his horse, but they can't find them. So what do they do?

They write to 221B Baker Street, London, of course – to ask for the help of the great detective, Sherlock Holmes.

Sister Love and Other Crime Stories

JOHN ESCOTT

Some sisters are good friends, some are not. Sometimes there is more hate in a family than there is love. Karin is beautiful and has lots of men friends, but she can be very unkind to her sister Marcia. Perhaps when they were small, there was love between them, but that was a long time ago.

They say that everybody has one crime in them. Perhaps they only take an umbrella that does not belong to them. Perhaps they steal from a shop, perhaps they get angry and hit someone, perhaps they kill . . .